Jessica V. Toussaint

BABYYY, YOU GOT THIS!

Legal Notice
Copyright 2024 – All Rights Reserved
The content in this book may not be reproduced, duplicated, or transmitted without written permission from the author or publisher. The author and publisher are not liable for any damages, reparation, or monetary loss due to information contained in this book. You are responsible for your own choices, actions, and results. This work is a piece of fiction. Names, characters, places, and incidents are either the product of the author's imagination or used fictitiously. Any resemblance to actual persons, living or dead, events, or locales is entirely coincidental.

All rights are provided by copyright law, including reproduction, distribution, and public display. Characters, names, and places are the sole property of the author and may not be reproduced, distributed, or used without written permission, except for quotations in a book review.

Unauthorized copying, reproduction, or distribution of this work, in whole or in part, without the author's permission is illegal and will be prosecuted to the full extent of the law.
For permissions, contact: hello@letsdreamencore.com

Disclaimer Notice
The information in this book is for general informational purposes only. Readers are advised to consult with a qualified professional for specific advice. The author and publisher disclaim any liability, loss, or risk incurred as a consequence of the use and application, directly or indirectly, of any information presented herein.
Every effort has been made to trace and credit copyright holders of material reproduced in this book. Any omissions brought to our notice will be rectified in subsequent editions.

Dedication

This book is dedicated to those who often struggle with who they are destined to be. Let this be a reminder that you are not alone in your journey, and within these pages, may you find solace, inspiration, and the courage to embrace the magnificent person you are destined to be. May these words serve as a guiding light, illuminating the path to self-discovery, self-love, and fulfilling your unique purpose.

Contents

Introduction 7
The Power of Decisions 9
Gifted and Talented 13
Acceptance 17
My Decision to Walk Away 21
I'm in Process 25
Going "All In" 29
Embracing Imperfections 33
You are Enough 37
Arise to Your Privilege 41
Unleashing Your Unique Brilliance 45
Healing Through Vulnerability 49
Embracing Your True Identity 53
Battling Insecurities 55
The Dark Room Experience 59
Trusting the Process 63
The Disruptive Power of Change 67
Shedding the Armor of Others 71
You are the Obstacle 75
The Pruning Season 79
Waiting Room 83

Beloved and Brave 87
Prayer for Renewed Minds 91
Final Thoughts 93

Introduction

"The wealthiest place in the world is not the gold mines of South America or the oil fields of Iraq or Iran. They are not the diamond mines of South Africa or the banks of the world. The wealthiest place on the planet is just down the road. It is the cemetery. There lie buried companies that were never started, inventions that were never made, bestselling books that were never written, and masterpieces that were never painted. In the cemetery is buried the greatest treasure of untapped potential." - Dr. Myles Monroe

Did you know that as humans, we process over 60,000 thoughts a day? Just imagine if we consciously rehearsed positive affirmations like "I am enough," "I have what it takes," and "I'm capable" repeatedly. Where would we be?

Picture a life where we are constantly affirming our worth and potential. Now, imagine stepping into any room with confidence and boldness, equipped with a mindset to pursue every opportunity that comes your way.

What would our lives look like if we fully embraced our identity and walked in the power that has been placed within us? Would we be further?

I invite you to explore, reflect and rediscover your true identity as we embark on the insightful journey along the pages of this book. Get ready to embark on a journey of self-discovery, acceptance and empowerment.

BABYYY, YOU GOT THIS!

The Power of Decisions

"The power of a single decision can change your destiny. Every choice shapes the narrative of your life, and in every decision, there is an opportunity for transformation." - Unknown

The decisions we make daily shapes our world; whether these decisions were made either by commission or omission, we're crafting the stories of our lives through our choices. From the moment we open our eyes, decisions await us, from hitting the snooze button to selecting our outfits. Every waking moment stands as an opportunity to carve out our destiny.

For instance, take a moment right now to pick up this book and invest in yourself – that, my friend, is a worthy decision. It's a conscious choice, signaling that you're ready to take a proactive role in your life. When we truly understand the extent of our control and influence, every choice before us becomes like a brushstroke, delicately painting our future.

Consider this book as not just a collection of words but a toolkit for empowerment. With each page turned, and each passing day, there is an opportunity to reflect, learn and grow. It is recognizing that every choice, regardless of its size, is a step toward the life you envision. Your decision to embark on this insightful journey is a declaration – a commitment to your personal development and the intentional shaping of your destiny.

Commit to unlearning ideas and notions embedded within you and be willing to examine your thought life. Be honest and vulnerable with yourself. Commit to reflection, and, most importantly, commit to application. Each day, we are blessed with an opportunity to start fresh and carry forward.

Commit to yourself.

Self-Reflection

1. What small decision can you make today that aligns with the life you envision for yourself?

   _____
   _____
   _____
   _____
   _____
   _____
   _____

2. In what areas of your life can you commit to unlearning old ideas and thought patterns to pave the way for personal growth?

   _____
   _____
   _____
   _____
   _____
   _____
   _____

Gifted and Talented

"A director is the captain of the ship; he gets the vision of the film much before anyone else can. While I want to experiment with characters, I know a good director means I am in safe hands." - Koel Mallick

We're not just players on the stage of life; we're the producers of our show, the masterminds behind the scenes. Picture it! Casting directors, scriptwriters, stagehands, and lighting directors all work together, crafting the storyline to the rhythm of your heartbeat. Our decisions shape the scenes, influencing how we are portrayed in this grand production.

Now, in this theatrical production called Life, we play a crucial role, but a divine director in the mix has already written the final script, He is the author and finisher of our faith. He takes the raw footage of our lives and skillfully weaves it into a seamless story. The Father doesn't shy away from the moments we might've preferred to edit out but has created a story that resonates profoundly with the audience. He is the real director who orchestrates it all for our benefit.

As we genuinely embrace this truth, we find a new stride in our story, recognizing that the journey has now begun. It's a reminder of the divine editing behind the scenes, turning our imperfections into a tale that impacts others in ways we may not fully comprehend.

Babyyy! Pick up your head, we can no longer hold our stories hostage in fear of what others may think about us. Instead, square your shoulders and look into the mirror. As you gaze at your reflection, you look at a miracle despite disappointments, challenges and momentary setbacks. While you may not be where you want to be, you are much further than where you started.

Self-Reflection

1. What decisions can you make today to actively contribute to crafting the storyline of your life in a way that aligns with your aspirations and values?

   _____
   _____
   _____
   _____
   _____
   _____
   _____
   _____

2. How can you embrace and take pride in your unique story, recognizing that even imperfections contribute to a narrative that can inspire and impact others?

   _____
   _____
   _____
   _____
   _____
   _____

Acceptance

"I know what I'm doing. I have it all planned out – plans to take care of you, not abandon you, plans to give you the future you hope for." - Jeremiah 29:11

Some bloopers, the imperfect shots, end up on the big screen. Ironically, these bad moments often hold the most significant impact on the audience. Our decisions and choices are the raw footage; the editor, in His wisdom, decides what shapes our storyline.

Every part, every scene, works together for our good in the end—a divine promise found in the pages of the Bible, God's love letter to us.

After reading this book, I pray that you feel secure sharing and owning every part of your story. The journey to accepting imperfection takes work. It requires standing at the crossroads, deciding whether to embrace every part of your story or hide certain aspects, succumbing to the pressure of attaining an unattainable perfection.

Consider this moment your yearly check-up, a time to sit with the most excellent physician, our Heavenly Father. As your story unfolds, recognize the impact of imperfect shots, the bloopers that shape your unique storyline. Allow His wisdom to guide your editing process and may accepting your imperfections lead to profound ownership of your story.

You are the billboard that will demonstrate what it looks like for God to turn our mess into a message.

Self-Reflection

1. How can you actively embrace and share the imperfect moments and bloopers in your life, trusting that they contribute to a larger, purposeful narrative crafted by a Divine Editor (God)?

_____
_____
_____
_____
_____
_____

2. Reflect on a specific aspect of your story that you may have been hesitant to own. How can you release the pressure of attaining perfection and find acceptance in sharing this part of your journey?

_____
_____
_____
_____
_____
_____

My Decision to Walk Away

"We all sense when we've overstayed our welcome. May God grant us the courage to recognize and embrace that moment."

In my journey, there came a crucial turning point, a moment that was etched in my mind when I decided to walk away from certain pieces of my life that no longer served me. It was far from an easy path; it led me through discomfort and uncertainty but marked the beginning of my transformative experience.

Sometimes in our lives, we know deep down that we've overstayed our welcome. Yet, instead of listening to the whispers of God to our soul and taking that necessary leap, we often choose to linger in comfort.

Human nature gravitates towards comfort, but beyond that lies purpose. Comfort may bring companions like average, complacency, and mediocrity, but if you're reading this, know that you've been called out for something greater.

Moving forward when we know it's time to move on might be challenging, but pursuing purpose is a journey worth taking.

So, let's embrace discomfort for growth and purpose, acknowledging that our decisions today are crafting the stories we'll share tomorrow. Too much is waiting on you.

This is a signal meant to give you a choice to see and do away with what no longer serves you right.

Self-Reflection

1. Reflect on a situation where you might sense the need to walk away. What whispers of discomfort or nudges from within signal that it's time for a change?

　_____
　_____
　_____
　_____
　_____
　_____
　_____

2. Consider the potential for growth and purpose beyond your comfort zone. What steps can you take today to embrace discomfort and make decisions that align with your greater calling and purpose?

　_____
　_____
　_____
　_____
　_____
　_____
　_____

I'm in Process.

"Don't count me out;
I'm in the middle of building something great."

According to the Oxford English Dictionary, "process is a continuous and regular action or succession of actions occurring or performed in a definite manner—often with reference to artificial or deliberate processes."

The process, for me, is a journey of shedding what was in order to embrace what is. When I reflect on yesterday, I ask myself, "Is this my best version? Have I stepped up to the plate? Have I done all it takes to bring the best out of myself?" It's an examination, a constant evolution toward becoming the most authentic and fulfilled version of who I aspire to be.

Everyone's process looks different, but we all should want the same outcome. The process can be messy, revealing the depths of our hearts. There are things we must unlearn.

When we accept the process, we give ourselves grace and let go of comparison, understanding that our journey and story are unique. We release the timeline, which we've placed on ourselves, and also, the ones others have placed on us too. We examine how we got to where we are. In the process, we explored the evidence of our accomplishments, countering lies.

In the process, we learn to love and accept ourselves. We commit to the work within us, investing time and energy in creating the life we have dreamed of and deserve. The process requires sacrifice and transparency. It also produces healing and restoration.

The next time someone tries to rush you into something you're not ready for, kindly remind them: 'Excuse me, I'm in process.' And remember, you are building something for the long run; as long as there's breathe in our lungs, there lies opportunity.

Self-Reflection

1. Consider aspects of your journey where you are "in process." What unlearning, forgiveness, or self-acceptance is required for your personal growth?

   _____
   _____
   _____
   _____
   _____
   _____
   _____

2. Reflect on the idea of embracing your unique process. How can you actively engage in self-improvement, release-imposed timelines, and invest in the work within you to create the life you dream of and deserve?

   _____
   _____
   _____
   _____
   _____
   _____

Going "All In"

*"Commit your work to the Lord,
and your plans will be established." - Proverbs 16:3*

Take a moment to imagine what life could look like if you were more committed to yourself. What dreams would you pursue? How would your relationships evolve? Picture yourself in these scenarios, sit in the stillness, and reflect on where you are. What did you feel in the moment of silence? What whispered in your spirit?

Permit yourself to fully commit to showing up for yourself. Confront the fears, doubts and hesitations that may linger in the background. Perhaps, it's the fear of failure, the uncertainty of the unknown or opinions about what others might think. Acknowledge these concerns without judgment. Understand that being "All in" doesn't necessarily mean having all the answers or ensuring success; it just means embracing the entire journey, with its highs and lows.

And remember to extend grace to yourself. Often, what holds us back from going all in is regret and comparison. How often have you thought, "By now, XYZ should have taken place"? Let it go! You are exactly where you are meant to be. Regret is a time waster. Forgive yourself, adjust your timeline, and get started. When negative thoughts arise, counter them with evidence of your achievements and successes.

You hold the power to shape your journey. Your path is uniquely yours, and every step forward is a victory.

Self-Reflection

1. During the moment of stillness, what aspirations surfaced in your thoughts? What dreams have been quietly calling you and patiently waiting for your response?

_____
_____
_____
_____
_____
_____

2. Reflect on the reasons holding you back from going "all in." What fears, doubts, or hesitations linger in the background? How can you overcome these obstacles to fully commit to showing up for yourself?

_____
_____
_____
_____
_____
_____

Embracing Imperfections

"To see the finished puzzle, we need every piece. Embrace and use each one-it's through this assembly that the full picture emerges."

I recall the Bible story of Moses grappling with a speech impediment and navigating through life with those challenges. David was a gifted king and worshipper but he was found in the fields where his family looked down on him. Peter, who walked with Jesus, had anger issues.

In a world that is engulfed with a sense of quickness to pass judgment, these people, seemingly disqualified by societal standards, didn't give up. Instead, they faced the court of public opinion, where guilt and flaws were glaringly apparent. Their limitations and humanity did not prevent their destiny. Nevertheless, God chose them to be architects of history and catalysts for change.

Consider this: You could have existed in any era, yet you're in this precise moment. God orchestrated this instance to remind you of God's immeasurable love and compassion, with your imperfections. Our flaws aren't stumbling blocks but vehicles through which God connects us to others. They are perpetual vehicles guiding us back to Him, a constant reminder of our unyielding dependence on His boundless grace.

So, my dear friend, embrace your flaws with the unwavering certainty that you are God's choice. He lovingly accepts every blemish, every wrinkle and every scar because you belong to Him. Your imperfections are not a sign of disqualification but a reminder of His perfection.

Self-Reflection

1. In what ways can you embrace your flaws as vehicles for connection and reminders of your worth?

   _____
   _____
   _____
   _____
   _____
   _____

2. Consider your imperfections – blemishes, wrinkles, scars. How can you shift your perspective to see them as a testament to your unique journey and a reminder of God's boundless grace?

   _____
   _____
   _____
   _____
   _____
   _____
   _____
   _____

You are Enough.

"But you are a chosen people, a royal priesthood, a holy nation, God's special possession, that you may declare the praises of him who called you out of darkness into his wonderful light." - 1 Peter 2:9

There was a season in my life where I poured every ounce of effort into trying to be "enough." What is "enough," you ask? It's that state of mind where I believed that if I secured the right job, surrounded myself with the right friends, moved in the right circles, and achieved the right weight. I thought, surely, this would make me 'feel good enough.' As time passed, I made strides in these areas while being persistent and empty. Have you ever felt that way? Be honest – it's just Jesus, you and me.

In my pursuit, I found myself mirroring Martha – consumed with work and accomplishments rather than resting at the feet of Jesus, like Mary.

The more I accomplished, the more frustration grew, until one day, it dawned on me that: my works could not validate me because God, our Father, had already done that. It was as if I was striving to earn something inherently mine. This was not something I could find in a person or thing, but only in my Heavenly Father.

His whispers echoed in my heart, reminding me that 'He knew me before I was formed in my mother's womb.' This statement brings tears because He was aware of my flaws even before I could recognize them and still chose me.

Flaws and all, you are undeniably enough. Our Father sees you and has marvelous plans for you. There's nothing else you need to do to earn His approval. You already have it! So, let's shift from striving to simply having faith that God knows exactly what He's doing with you, for you, and through you.

Self-Reflection

1. Reflect on the pursuit of being 'enough' in your own life. Have you ever felt the persistent emptiness that comes from striving for external validation?

   _____
   _____
   _____
   _____
   _____
   _____
   _____

2. How can shifting your perspective, as mentioned in the passage, impact your sense of self-worth?

   _____
   _____
   _____
   _____
   _____
   _____
   _____
   _____

Arise to Your Privilege

*"If a light is hidden in the darkness,
are you still seen?"*

"**GET OVER IT!**" was the blunt conversation I had with myself when I realized that I was living beneath my privilege. Take a moment and ponder: are you doing the same? Too often, our lack of self-worth propels us into situations that fail to reflect the greatness within us.

I vividly recall when I offered top-notch services for a wedding, only to be met with disappointing responses. It hit me: how could someone value my worth when I don't value myself? People value what they invest in... time, talent and resources, so often, we give so much away that we start to lose value.

One day, while spending time with God, I had a revelation: that there is so much in store for me once I commit to living above my privilege. If I honor Him by living up to His standard, not aimlessly wandering and giving away what He has blessed me with, then I will be in purpose.

Stewardship is our responsibility. Will we be like David and not be confident and trust that God has called us, or will we be like Peter, who doesn't look or sound like everybody but has a purpose? Not every opportunity is the right opportunity, but when we downplay our contributions, we downplay our Father.

It's time to confidently take our seat at the table, knowing that if God brought us to that opportunity, relationship or position, we have what it takes to thrive.

Self-Reflection

1. Reflect on a time when you may have devalued your worth or capabilities. How did this impact the way others perceived you, and what lessons can be drawn from this experience of recognizing and embracing your privilege?

   _____
   _____
   _____
   _____
   _____
   _____

2. Consider the concept of stewardship mentioned in the passage. How can you be more purposeful with your time, talent, and resources?

   _____
   _____
   _____
   _____
   _____
   _____
   _____

Unleashing Your Unique Brilliance

"Compromising begins with one decision that leads to a bill we never intended to pay."

It's okay to color outside of the lines. Whew, take a breath! You cannot expect others to see in you what you refuse to take seriously. You don't need permission to embrace what makes you different; in fact, that difference is what gives you an edge.

Sometimes, we try to dilute the very thing God has placed in us and deny the same thing He wants to use. Our lives start to glisten once we accept Him and surrender to His will. We become the billboard that shines bright in the middle of a busy world while God reflects His image on Earth. It may sound amazing and overwhelming simultaneously, but just know that once He finishes the polishing, you will see the sovereignty of God.

I remember trying to dilute my potency, inherited from God our Heavenly Father, to accommodate others. That experience taught me the cost of compromising something I didn't even earn or buy. It can leave us crippled, defenseless, void and we may lose our voice.

We have the responsibility to guard our minds and hearts, not allowing them to become a garden for the enemy or others' opinions to plant things that do not align with God's word concerning us. Such influences will only lead us to dim our light and dull our edge, making us the opposite of God's intent for us.

Beloved, it's time to take back your mind and guard your heart. God has given us the responsibility and authority to govern. He has already made us free through the sacrifice of Jesus Christ. The power lies within us; **it's time to activate it.**

Self-Reflection

1. Consider a time when you may have felt the need to dilute your uniqueness to accommodate others. What were the consequences, and how did it impact your sense of self?

_____
_____
_____
_____
_____
_____
_____
_____

2. Reflect on the value of embracing and unleashing your unique brilliance as a reflection of God's design for you.

_____
_____
_____
_____
_____
_____
_____

Healing Through Vulnerability

"Pain serves as a poignant indicator that opportunities lie ahead, echoing the breath within our bodies. Amidst the struggles, the pulse of life propels us toward renewal, whispering the promise of new opportunities waiting to unfold."

Sometimes, pain leaves you paralyzed. It makes you feel misunderstood and alone, causing you to build walls. The sharpness of pain serves as a reminder of the dormant emptiness inside. Yet, in its vulnerability, there lies the potential for growth and greater happiness.

Pain leads to memories and triggers, unveiling the raw truth. It's a journey through vulnerability, alarming in its nakedness yet, enabling us to rebuild and continue our story. The bar isn't perfection but progression.

Vulnerability is the key to security in Christ. Honest conversations with ourselves become crucial – who told you that you were not good enough? How does it manifest? When did you notice its impact? These questions help us to own our truth.

Being vulnerable allows us to share with God the depths of our pain. It invites the Healer to fill the gaps only He can mend. God waits for us to show Him the scars so He can nurse us back together.

It's time to come to the Healer. He desires to go to the depths of our hearts and souls, mending what is broken. As a gentleman, He awaits our invitation.

It's time to take down the guards, feel and process. Let the tears well up; enter the hospital room and let Him perform surgery. It might be challenging to share your heart with those who don't understand the unspoken pain, but we have a high priest who understands our weaknesses. He faced the same tests and remained without sin.

Your healing begins **today**.

Self-Reflection

1. Consider the role of vulnerability in overcoming pain and fostering growth. How can embracing vulnerability lead to healing and a renewed sense of purpose?

   _____
   _____
   _____
   _____
   _____
   _____

2. Explore the concept of having honest conversations with yourself and with God about your pain. How can you create a space for God to heal the broken areas of your life by inviting Him into the depths of your heart and soul?

   _____
   _____
   _____
   _____
   _____
   _____
   _____

Embracing Your True Identity

"Just as the caterpillar transforms into a butterfly, our journey involves unraveling self-deception."

There are moments when our inadequacies weigh heavily on our hearts, plunging us into cycles rooted in the belief that we are damaged goods. Unconsciously, we've embraced this falsehood, distorting our perspective through dirty lenses.

These lenses not only amplify insecurities but also intensify the impact of trauma, turning rejection into a dwelling place within our hearts. It's a journey of self-deception that we must unravel to see our worth.

The enemy invades our thoughts, shapes our environment, and persuades us to believe that we don't have what it takes. When you cry, there is a seed hidden deep within. The seed germinates, producing assurance and security, reminding us of our flaws and all that we are loved, valued, cherished, and, most importantly, our name is written on His heart.

This assurance should give you a renewed strength to stay on the journey, hoping that one day, you'll wake up and believe that you are enough. But it takes work; we must commit to the journey each day and moment. **You are worth it!**

Self-Reflection

1. Reflect on when you felt weighed down by inadequacies and distorted perspectives. How can you identify and unravel moments of self-deception in your journey towards recognizing your true worth?

   _____
   _____
   _____
   _____
   _____
   _____
   _____

2. Consider the impact of external influences and negative thoughts on your self-perception. How can you combat the enemy's tactics that undermine your worth?

   _____
   _____
   _____
   _____
   _____
   _____
   _____

Battling Insecurities

"What voice will you listen to?"

Take a moment to delve into my transparent reflections.

Throughout the week, the chorus echoing within me has been that I am not good enough, unworthy of the seat I occupy. I've confronted the echoes of my past, an old version rising to challenge my progress.

Yet, I wage war against these insidious thoughts, refusing to let them define my reality. Instead, I unearth evidence of my triumphs, affirming that I have overcome, possess the strength required, and, above all, that God, my Father, and has justified me.

I swap out the cassette of comparison and defeat, replacing it with the voice of God. In moments when I feel lost, He becomes my anchor, guiding me back to certainty. The still, small voice reassures me that I am destined to endure.

At the crossroads of faith and defeat, I opt for faith. I choose to believe in the untold chapters of my story, recognizing my purpose and trusting in divinely guided footsteps. Yet, as my heart encounters vulnerability and fear, I am reminded that beyond it lies something greater.

Extending my hands, I pleaded with the Lord, 'Help me get there!'

I share this transparent moment to underscore that the journey toward wholeness is a daily, courageous endeavor. The inner struggles may try to convince us otherwise, but I assure you that God meets us at our point of need. We belong to Him. It's time to surrender and return, for He awaits us with the value and validation we seek.

Self-Reflection

1. Reflect on a recent moment when you confronted feelings of unworthiness or inadequacy. How did you overcome these thoughts, and what evidence of your triumphs did you uncover to affirm your strength and worth?

_____
_____
_____
_____
_____
_____

2. In what ways can faith guide you through moments of vulnerability and fear, trusting in the untold chapters of your story and divine guidance?

_____
_____
_____
_____
_____
_____

The Dark Room Experience

"A diamond's creation requires immense pressure and intense temperatures to reach its highest potential. Without enduring the adversity and pressure of its environment, the diamond would never become the treasure it was meant to be. May the changes you grow through bring incredible value in helping you forge a remarkable and multi-faceted life." - Susan C. Young

In a world saturated with misleading images and videos, it's crucial to recognize that success is comparable to a photograph developed in a dark room. Success, when treated with precision and care, relies on the meticulous effort and attention to detail within that concealed space. Do not be deceived, and never underestimate the significance of the dark room.

The dark room is a precious time, a crucial phase where the right solutions perfect the image. Taking the image outside the dark room prematurely risks losing the photographer's quality, accuracy, and, in some cases, the image altogether. Embrace your darkroom experience, for in it, you emerge as God intended – in time, with great quality and a picture that glorifies Him.

In the day and age of instant gratification, we despise the dark room innately. The dark room calls us to concentrate, to take our time, and to let patience have its perfect work. But it's in the dark room where we see the beauty of the process. In the dark room, we see a blank page transform into a beautiful work of art.

Remain focused, knowing a photograph cannot remain in the dark forever. Your image was created for a reason, and you hold significance. Change your perspective on the darkroom experience, maximize the journey, and refrain from rushing the process.

Keep your eyes fixed on the final results, envision the image before it becomes visible. My dear, you are valuable. Persevere the process, for in due time; you will witness the emergence of a fully developed piece of art – called **YOU**.

Self-Reflection

1. How do you perceive the "dark room" experiences in your life, where patience and precision are required for growth and success?

   _____
   _____
   _____
   _____
   _____
   _____
   _____

2. How might reframing your perspective on patience and process positively impact your overall growth?

   _____
   _____
   _____
   _____
   _____
   _____
   _____

Trusting the Process

"Trust God from the bottom of your heart; don't try to figure out everything on your own. Listen for God's voice in everything you do, everywhere you go; he's the one who will keep you on track."
- Proverbs 3:5-6

Today, I heard the Lord's gentle whisper urging you to trust Him completely. He calls for your heart, your insecurities, and your plans to be placed in His hands. Involve Him in every aspect of your life, consulting Him in your daily plans. He longs to be a part of your journey, desiring to hear from you daily.

Negativity can take root when we are too busy with everything else and forget to involve God in our day-to-day affairs. Just as a plant needs proper nutrients, water and sunlight to thrive, we too, need to be intentional about our wholeness. Partner with God in this journey.

Remember, trust is the prerequisite for faith. But let's be real; trust is scary and complicated, especially when you can't see the answer, the solution, and you don't know what is next. But that is when trust steps in and reminds you that you are not in this alone and that you have a track record of not failing.

Trust requires walking through the pain, acknowledging it, but affirming that despite the challenges, you can trust God, our Heavenly Father. He has brought you this far, and He knows every detail about you, and still chooses you. Trust means that we relinquish our control, knowing that we will be okay and covered.

Trust means when challenged to walk away from certain details, we know we are not missing out. Trust God, trust the process. Trust Him enough to bare your soul, reveal your secrets, and trace the origins of your insecurities. He is the Healer of the brokenhearted, binding up wounds with His love.

It's time to trust what's inside of you. Remove the cassette, change your tune, and lean into it. You can be trusted. Trust your Heavenly Father. This trust marks the beginning of your journey to wholeness.

Self-Reflection

1. Reflect on a specific area of your life where trust in God has played a significant role.

_____
_____
_____
_____
_____
_____
_____

2. How has trusting God's guidance and plan brought positive outcomes or growth in that particular aspect?

_____
_____
_____
_____
_____
_____
_____
_____

The Disruptive Power of Change

"Behold, I make all things new." - Revelation 21:5

Have you ever invested in others, cheered for their victories, and celebrated their growth? Today, the spotlight shifts and it's your time to take center stage. The journey to self-discovery awaits, and you don't have to tread this path alone.

Just like David faced Goliath, it's time to confront the giants that threaten your peace and worth. The Holy Spirit stands ready to lead and guide, offering the strength needed to slay the challenges that came to slay you.

This is your moment to shed the behaviors that no longer serve you—starting with the eradication of negative self-talk. Change begins with that first courageous step, even if fear lingers in the shadows. Remember, different results require different actions.

Change, though disruptive and radical, is the catalyst for true growth and development. It invites you to discard the opinions of others, change your wardrobe of thoughts, and alter your perspective in the pursuit of becoming new.

It's time to embrace the discomfort of change because you are worth it. This transformation is not earned but freely given, a precious gift from our loving Father. As you take that first step, know that a new and empowered version of yourself is waiting to emerge.

Self-Reflection

1. Identify one area in your life where change is needed for personal growth.

   _____
   _____
   _____
   _____
   _____
   _____
   _____

2. What specific negative self-talk or behavior can you courageously confront and begin to shed to initiate positive change?

   _____
   _____
   _____
   _____
   _____
   _____
   _____

Shedding the Armor of Others

"Everything you need lives on the inside."

Let me remind you of the epic tale of David and Goliath—a giant Philistine who tormented the people of Israel for forty days until a shepherd boy named; David stepped forward. Before this iconic battle, David faced skepticism and doubt from those around him. But his lifework had uniquely prepared him for this moment.

When David approached King Saul, the natural inclination was to dress him in the king's armor. However, David quickly realized that he couldn't carry the weight of another man's armor into battle. What if he had accepted that burden? Would history have been made? David, undeterred by the lack of faith around him, chose to face the giant in his way.

The lesson for us here is profound. Often, we wear the armor that others have placed upon us—labels, opinions, and judgments that aren't our own. Our struggles with feeling unworthy are often entwined with the narratives others have woven about us. But my dear, the only voices that truly matter are those of our Heavenly Father and our own.

It's time to strip away the perspectives others have imposed on us courageously.

David wasn't concerned with the opinions of those around him because he knew he already had everything he needed within himself.

Let's take back our minds and hearts, tearing down the strongholds that have confined us. Just like David, be assured that you have everything within you to face and conquer the giants in your life. You were born for this moment of triumph.

Self-Reflection

1. Reflect on the armor of others you might be carrying—labels, opinions, or judgments that don't align with your identity. How can you courageously shed these external influences to embrace your authentic self?

   _____
   _____
   _____
   _____
   _____
   _____

2. Consider a specific area in your life where you've allowed others' perspectives to shape your narrative. How can you follow David's example and confidently face the challenges in your way, trusting in the strength and resources within you?

   _____
   _____
   _____
   _____
   _____

You are the Obstacle.

"I can do all things through Christ who strengthens me."- Philippians 4:13

Often, we find ourselves blaming others for the way we are. Trauma is real, and things happen outside our control, but we have the power to determine how they play out in our lives.

Consider two women who have experienced sexual assault. As a result, one takes the path of being an advocate for women who have been abused. At the same time, the other becomes sexually promiscuous to numb the pain: same instance, same horror, but both with very different responses. The same applies to us; what happened to us does not have to dictate where we choose to live.

I remember trying to put this book together, repeatedly self-sabotaging by making excuses, pushing back timelines, and then realizing, 'Girl, you are the obstacle.' You determine whether this ever gets out to the world.

Our greatest fight and opponent are within us. No one can talk us into or out of something more than ourselves. If we know areas where we are weak, we must arm ourselves with the resources, tools, and accountability we need.

You are not what happened to you but the sum total of your decisions. It starts with one step: admitting that we are the problem. Yet, because we are the problem, we are also the solution. It's time to make up our minds that we are worth betting on and worth the investment.

Self-Reflection

1. How have you seen instances in your life where your response to challenges or trauma played a significant role in shaping your outcomes?

   _____
   _____
   _____
   _____
   _____
   _____
   _____

2. In what ways have you recognized self-sabotaging behaviors within yourself, and how can you shift your mindset to overcome them and realize your potential?

   _____
   _____
   _____
   _____
   _____
   _____
   _____

The Pruning Season

"To everything, there is a season, a time for every purpose under heaven: A time to be born, and a time to die; a time to plant, and a time to pluck what is planted; A time to kill, and a time to heal; a time to break down, and a time to build up."
- Ecclesiastes 3:1-3

When the pruning season arrives, it makes no apologies. It is abrupt, offering no consolation or constellation, and if I'm honest, it hurts. I believed I was on the path to a promotion, but out of nowhere, I was gut-punched!

I remember orchestrating my pity party, tainted with shame and too afraid to extend invitations. Countless interviews felt like performances, with people deciding if I was good enough.

Yet, through God's whispers and the support of my community, I realized that God strategically put me on pause to reflect on my journey. He unveiled how much I had placed my value in others rather than in myself, leading me to the examination table in order to see the center of my heart. It was a humbling experience. I recognized that pride had driven me, convincing me that my successes were solely in my strength and intellect. But in that moment, I was humbled and reminded that He gifted me and would open the next door.

This divine pause prompted a realignment. After popping the balloons and discarding the decorations, I recalled His whispered promises that the cares of life had tried to snatch. When we think of pruning, it's associated with cutting, a process no one enjoys. Yet, in these strategic cuts, the plant grows stronger, reaching its optimum.

To everything, there is a season. At the end of my pruning season, I gained the time I was missing, the rest I needed, strengthened relationships, revived dormant dreams, gained clarity, and deepened my faith. When the next position arrived, it was precisely what I desired. Disregard the whispers of lies telling you that you're missing out. My dear, you are right where you are supposed to be, and after this, there will be glory, **I promise.**

Self-Reflection

1. Reflect on a time in your life when you experienced a "pruning season" – a period of unexpected challenges or setbacks. How did you initially react to it, and what lessons did you eventually learn from that experience?

   _____
   _____
   _____
   _____
   _____
   _____

2. Consider the metaphor of pruning in the context of personal growth. Are there areas in your life where you feel the need for pruning, letting go, or realignment?

   _____
   _____
   _____
   _____
   _____
   _____

Waiting Room

"Great things take place in the waiting room."

In the waiting room of life, I often find myself suspended between two worlds. I can envision the promise that exists, yet my current reality bears no evidence of it. There's an internal grumble, a yearning for a new day—the day when things will finally change. Perhaps, you can relate to this sense of anticipation.

This space, this waiting room, is where we reside when the goal or dream seems just out of reach. What unfolds in the waiting room is intricately tied to our response. It's a space of development, unique for each person. Take, for example, a woman seeking marriage; her waiting room is a single life. For a couple, the waiting room might be the journey toward conceiving their first child. For another, it could be the anticipation of a long-awaited job offer.

Take the time to tune in to the subtle messages that this waiting room carries. What is life trying to communicate in this pause? Is it urging you to be patient, cultivate resilience, or perhaps redirect your focus? The answers may not immediately present themselves but trust that they will eventually reveal themselves.

This waiting room is more than just a pause; it's a transformative space. It's where we define ourselves, nurture our dreams, and prepare for the promises that lie ahead. Embracing the waiting room requires a conscious choice to engage in internal work, appreciating the process, and trusting that, in due time, the door will open to the next chapter of our lives.

Self-Reflection

1. In your current waiting room experience, what subtle messages do you sense life is trying to communicate?

   _____
   _____
   _____
   _____
   _____
   _____
   _____

2. How can you actively engage in internal work to nurture personal growth and resilience?

   _____
   _____
   _____
   _____
   _____
   _____
   _____

Beloved and Brave

"Bravery is not the absence of fear but the triumph over it. It's marked by the courage to face uncertainties, leave the past behind, and move forward into the possibilities that await on the other side." - Nelson Mandela

The Bible, our sacred love letter from God, resounds with His unwavering affirmation that we are His cherished creation—crafted in His image. As I pen this down, overwhelmed by the realization that we are not orphans but beloved by a Heavenly Father passionately in love with us, let's delve into the transformative story of Rahab.

Consider Rahab, a woman labeled by society as a harlot, judged for her actions rather than her heart. Yet, beneath her surface, she possessed faith and bravery that led her to protect two spies, ultimately transforming her from harlot to heroine.

In the same way, despite your perceived 'condition,' known only to you or perhaps even to others, remember that you have a God who unequivocally chooses you. Rahab's shortcomings did not disqualify her; she was spared. But she had to revisit history, recognizing God's faithfulness and trust in that more than her fear.

Your journey, flaws and all is purposeful; you didn't arrive here accidentally or alone. It's time to follow Rahab's courageous footsteps, leaving the past behind and moving forward. The choice lies between freedom and entanglement.

Let's be brave enough to believe in ourselves, unlocking not only our potential but also impacting those connected to us. The other side awaits, filled with possibilities only bravery can unfold.

Self-Reflection

1. Rahab's story involves a transformation from societal judgment to heroism. In what ways can you embrace the assurance of being beloved by a Heavenly Father despite any societal labels or judgments?

   _____
   _____
   _____
   _____
   _____
   _____

2. Think about a past event or aspect of your life that you might need to leave behind in order to move forward. How can revisiting that history and recognizing God's faithfulness contribute to your growth and freedom?

   _____
   _____
   _____
   _____
   _____
   _____

Prayer for Renewed Minds

"He hears our prayers. Speak to Him; He's listening."

God our Father, we lay bare the sentiments of our hearts. In moments of inadequacy, we find solace in Your unwavering love. Without You, we are like sinking ships, lacking direction. Yet, Your love—an everlasting embrace—accepts and cherishes every imperfection.

Thank You, Lord, for never giving up on us and for loving us beyond our thoughts or current situation. Help us to see ourselves through Your eyes, believe in Your unfailing love, and ignite the flames of our faith. Unlike man, You neither lie nor disappoint. Your breath fills our lungs; we exist because of You. Suicidal attempts, low self-esteem, depression, and self-hatred couldn't prevent us from being here, a testament to Your grace.

We plead for Your intervention, Lord. Remove the scales from our eyes, renew our minds, and reassure us of the worth You have already bestowed upon us. Tear down negative mindsets and perform the surgery that turns hearts of stone into flesh. Fill the voids in our hearts with Your Spirit, entering the secret places within. Surround us with relationships that feed our souls.

We yearn for Your presence, desperate for change. Transform the way we speak to ourselves, reshape our thoughts, and redefine our self-perception. We dedicate our lives back to You, the Manufacturer, the Author of our Faith.

Our thoughts and opinions are surrendered to Your will and Your way. We release our timeline, setting aside comparison. Align us with all that You have spoken about us in Your Word. Renovate our minds. We are Your children, prized possessions, lenders, not borrowers—the apple of Your eye. We belong to You. We are enough. Help us believe it deeply enough to walk in this truth.

In the mighty name of Jesus, we pray. **Amen**.

Final Thoughts

Congratulations on concluding this transformative journey! But let me be clear: you're not just closing a book; you're turning the page to a brand-new chapter in your life. Embrace the courage within you to step into the endless possibilities that await, leaving behind the echoes of self-doubt and the toxic game of comparison.

My deepest hope is that the words within these pages have stirred something profound within you. I want them to be more than just words; I want them to propel you into decisive action.

No longer tether yourself to the excuses of yesterday; rise above the fear and hopelessness that attempt to paralyze you. It's time to cast off the perceptions that once held you captive and, instead, take on the strength to become.

You are at your absolute best when you wholeheartedly embrace the person you are destined to be. Nurture the seeds within you with intentional care. Extend forgiveness to others for their wrongs, freeing yourself from the burden of resentment. And don't forget to grant yourself the grace of forgiveness for your own mistakes and decisions; release the weight that hinders your progress.

As you embark on the journey ahead, trust the process, knowing that you walk hand in hand with our Heavenly Father. External opinions or past narratives do not dictate your worth. You are a masterpiece in progress, a story unfolding in divine timing.

In closing, let this reflection be more than just words on a page; let it be a catalyst for bold action. Allow it to ignite a renewed sense of purpose, propelling you to step into the person you are destined to become with boldness. Remember, this journey doesn't end here; it's an ongoing, courageous endeavor towards wholeness.

I'm rooting for you every step of the way, and always remember' **BABYYY, YOU GOT THIS**!

www.ingramcontent.com/pod-product-compliance
Lightning Source LLC
LaVergne TN
LVHW050841080526
838202LV00009B/309